SURPRISED BY
HOPE

Participant's Guide

SURPRISED BY
HOPE

✝

Rethinking Heaven, the Resurrection, and the Mission of the Church

Six Sessions

N. T. WRIGHT

with Kevin and Sherry Harney

ZONDERVAN®

ZONDERVAN.com/
AUTHORTRACKER
follow your favorite authors

ZONDERVAN

Surprised by Hope Participant's Guide
Copyright © 2010 by N. T. Wright

Requests for information should be addressed to:

Zondervan, *Grand Rapids, Michigan* 49530

ISBN 978-0-310-32470-6

All Scripture quotations are taken from the Holy Bible, *New International Version*®, *NIV*®. Copyright © 1973, 1978, 1984 by Biblica, Inc.™ Used by permission of Zondervan. All rights reserved worldwide.

Any Internet addresses (websites, blogs, etc.) and telephone numbers printed in this book are offered as a resource. They are not intended in any way to be or imply an endorsement by Zondervan, nor does Zondervan vouch for the content of these sites and numbers for the life of this book.

All rights reserved. No part of this publication may be reproduced, stored in a retrieval system, or transmitted in any form or by any means—electronic, mechanical, photocopy, recording, or any other—except for brief quotations in printed reviews, without the prior permission of the publisher.

Cover design: Rob Monacelli
Cover photography: Ilona Wellmann/Trevillion Images
Interior design: Sherri Hoffman

Printed in the United States of America

09 10 11 12 13 14 15 • 24 23 22 21 20 19 18 17 16 15 14 13 12 11 10 9 8 7 6 5 4 3 2 1

† CONTENTS

✝
A WORD FROM N. T. WRIGHT

What are we waiting for? And what are we going to do about it in the meantime?

Those two questions shape the focus and direction of this DVD study. First, it is about the ultimate hope held out in the Christian gospel: the hope, that is, for salvation, resurrection, eternal life, and the cluster of other things that go with them. Second, it is about the discovery of hope within the present world; about the practical ways in which hope can come alive for communities and individuals who for whatever reason may lack it. And it is about the ways in which embracing the first can and should generate and sustain the second.

Most people, in my experience—including many Christians—don't know what the ultimate Christian hope really is. Most people—again, sadly, including many Christians—don't expect Christians to have much to say about hope within the present world. Most people don't imagine that these two could have anything to do with each other. Hence the title of this study: hope comes as a surprise, at several levels at once.

This study will help establish a foundation of practical and even political theology—of, that is, Christian reflection on the nature of the task we face as we seek to bring God's kingdom to bear on the real and painful world in which we live.

With that in mind, a disclaimer is in order. I am not a politician, though it is true that by virtue of my office as Bishop of Durham I am a member of the British House of Lords. I have neither run for public office nor campaigned actively—in terms of the sheer hard work of speaking, writing, marching, cajoling—for many of the causes in which I believe. I have tried to put my shoulder to the wheel by other means. But the subjects in which I have specialized, and the pastoral situations I now face every day in a diocese where some suffer severely from the faceless cruelties of the last fifty years, have forced me to think through some of what a Christian should be saying and thinking about rediscovering hope in the public and political world.

As I have done so, I have found these two themes of hope, again and again, joining themselves together. Hope is about what lies ahead and is promised by a God who loves to bring hope to each one of us. It is also about the kingdom of God breaking into our present-day realities and hope spilling out into the world today. These two ideas and realities are bound together and can't be separated, as hard as some might try.

As we dig into this study it is helpful to remember that all language about the future is simply a set of signposts pointing into a fog. We see through a glass darkly, says St. Paul as he peers toward what lies ahead. All our language about future states of the world and of ourselves consists of complex pictures that may or may not correspond very well to the ultimate reality. But that doesn't mean it's anybody's guess or that every opinion is as good as every other one.

And—supposing someone came forward out of the fog to meet us? That, of course, is the central though often ignored Christian belief. As you enter into this study of hope, it is my prayer that you will see Jesus inviting you to experience and extend hope in this world, and that you will feel him walking at your side along the way.

N. T. Wright

†

The quotations interspersed throughout this participant's guide are excerpts from the book *Surprised by Hope: Rethinking Heaven, the Resurrection, and the Mission of the Church* by N. T. Wright (Harper One, 2008).

HOPE FOR THE WORLD

God wants his people to experience hope and to share it with the world. Hope that has world transforming power is more than just anticipation of what God will do in the future. It is the coming of God's kingdom here on earth ... today.

✝ INTRODUCTION

This DVD study series, based on N. T. Wright's book of the same name, invites us to look closer and think deeper. Wright has a beautiful way of pointing to the familiar and helping us see things we never noticed before.

There are words in the Christian vocabulary that can feel familiar, almost a bit worn. Words like *heaven, resurrection, salvation,* and *the church* should stir our imagination and cause our heart to race, but often they can feel mundane.

In these six sessions you will be invited to take a fresh new look at the theological landscape of the Christian faith. N. T. Wright will be your tour guide. Along the way those familiar landmarks, locations, and ideas will begin to take on new meaning that will do more than stir your heart ... they will transform your life!

The first destination on this journey is the place where the Christian hope is born. What is the source of our hope? Can the hope found in Jesus really transform our lives and the world in which we live? And, how can those who follow Christ bring his light to a hope-starved world?

> "God's kingdom" in the preaching of Jesus refers not to postmortem destiny, not to our escape from this world into another one, but to God's sovereign rule coming "on earth as it is in heaven."

✝ TALK ABOUT IT

How might living with the assurance and hope of heaven, and having confidence in the resurrection, move us to action and bring hope right where we live today?

> What we say about death and resurrection gives shape and color to everything else. If we are not careful, we will offer merely a "hope" that is no longer a surprise, no longer able to transform lives and communities in the present, no longer generated by the resurrection of Jesus himself and looking forward to the promised new heavens and new earth.

✝ DVD TEACHING NOTES

As you watch the DVD teaching segment for session one, featuring N. T. Wright, use the following outline to record anything that stands out to you.

People all around of the world are asking, "Is there any hope?" and they do so with good reason! Two particular ways that people can go astray:

- The "secret code" approach

- The "escape the world" approach

The biblical vision for this world and the future

What the Bible means and does not mean when it talks about judging the world

The Gospels and Jesus' teaching about hope and God's kingdom

The conflict between the message of God's kingdom coming and the presiding powers of Jesus' day (religious and political)

The apostle Paul's vision of hope

A good definition of being the church

> "Thy kingdom come, on earth as in heaven," remains one of the most powerful and revolutionary sentences we can ever say. As I see it, the prayer was powerfully answered at the first Easter and will finally be answered fully when heaven and earth are joined in the new Jerusalem. Easter was when Hope in person surprised the whole world by coming forward from the future into the present.

✝ DVD DISCUSSION

1. Tell a story from your personal life, church life, or national history, where a person of hope stood up for others during a hard time and helped bring hope back to the people.

2. N. T. Wright lives and ministers in a region where there is potential for hopelessness and fatalism. Name places in your community or country where hope seems to have run out and that desperately need a fresh infusion of the hope that only God can bring.

3. If someone asked you, "What is the hope of the Christian faith?" what would you answer?

4. Wright reflects on a series of happenings around the world that have led to a sense of hopelessness for many people—including floods, famines, disasters, wars, economic crises, and political upheaval. What happenings in your lifetime have stripped away people's hope, and why do these events have such a devastating impact?

5. Wright talks about two particular mistakes that occur when it comes to understanding the Bible and hope. How have you seen the "secret code" approach and the "escape the world" approach lived out by people in the church?

> Christmas itself has now far outstripped Easter in popular culture as the real celebratory center of the Christian year—a move that completely reverses the New Testament's emphasis.

6. Though the Bible clearly offers the hope of heaven and the certainty of a future resurrection, it does *not* teach that God will one day throw this world into some celestial trash heap. Read the following passages and discuss how God sees the world:

   • Psalm 96:11–13

- Isaiah 11:1–9

- Revelation 21:1–5

7. How does Wright's understanding of judgment in Psalm 96:13—that God is coming to judge the earth with righteousness and truth—push back against the idea that God is angry at the world and ready to burn it up and throw it away?

8. In the Sermon on the Mount, Jesus teaches his followers to pray, "Our Father in heaven, hallowed be your name, your kingdom come, your will be done, on earth as it is in heaven" (Matthew 6:9–10). What do you think Jesus is asking us to pray, and how does this connect with the hope God wants to bring to this world?

9. Wright explains from the book of Acts how both the Jewish and pagan powers of the day were shocked and pushed back against the idea that a new kingdom was coming into this world. Early

believers were forced to decide if they would follow the existing power systems in the world (and their way of doing things) or God's ways and his kingdom vision. How might next week look different if you fully embraced a "God's kingdom come" approach to living?

10. Wright suggests that a good definition of *the church* would be: "people who gather together to share hope and be people of hope in the world." What do you think of this definition of the church? How might the activity of your local congregation change if you actually functioned with a profound sense that one of your primary callings is to be a community of hope right where God has placed you?

Most people have little or no idea what the word *resurrection* actually means or why Christians say they believe it.

If your group has time, you may choose to watch the bonus section of the DVD for session one now. (If not, consider viewing it on your own or as a group as part of your between-sessions activities.) Here are some reflection questions for the bonus section:

What are some of the ways the church has brought pain and heart-ache to the world?

How can we confess this, with authentic humility, to God and the world?

How has the church served and loved the world in ways that have brought healing, grace, and hope?

How can we celebrate these things and continue with this legacy?

Take time as a group to pray in some of the following directions:

- Ask God to help you live with a confidence that his hope is yours, both now and forever.
- Pray for a fresh new understanding that God wants to see his kingdom come on this earth as it is in heaven.
- Pray for the Holy Spirit to move you, your small group, and your church into the world with actions of love and hope that reveal the presence of God.

> Heaven, in the Bible, is not a future destiny but the other, hidden, dimension of our ordinary life—God's dimension, if you like. God made heaven and earth; at the last he will remake both and join them together forever.

✝
BETWEEN SESSIONS

Personal Reflection

Think about where God has placed you. God wants to bring his hope through you to the places you shop, dine, work, play, and live. At the start of the session N. T. Wright spoke of the needs in his community, the changing economy, and the pain people are facing. Reflect on the people in your life and what they are facing. Ask God to use you as a beacon of hope in each of these relationships.

Personal Action

Take a walk or drive around your community ... the place God has planted you. Pray for eyes to see the pain, loss, and hopelessness that can saturate our world. Actually ask the Holy Spirit to help you see beyond the physical to begin perceiving with the eyes of Jesus. As you see and feel the reality of what so many people face each day, pray for the kingdom of God to begin breaking into these places and lives. If you feel a prompting of the Spirit to take some kind of action in response to this exercise ... act on it!

Group Engagement

Wright told a story about a church in his community that started a school for people who had great physical and mental challenges. What is one action of hope your group can take in the next month to bring heaven to earth right in your community? If possible, discuss and decide this *before* your next group gathering, in order to get the activity on everyone's schedule.

Prayer Direction

- Pray for eyes to see the needs of the community around you.
- Ask the Spirit to soften your heart to those who are hurting and needy.
- Pray for your local church to become a beacon of hope in your community.
- Pray that God's kingdom will come and his will be done in your life, home, and community ... as it is in heaven.

Recommended Reading

As you reflect on what you have learned in this session you may want to read chapters 1 and 2 of the book *Surprised by Hope*, by N. T. Wright. Then, in preparation for session two, you may want to read chapters 3 and 4 as well.

Journal, Reflections, and Notes

_____

_____

_____

_____

_____

_____

_____

_____

_____

_____

_____

_____

_____

_____

_____

_____

_____

_____

THE HOPE OF THE RESURRECTION

The hope of the resurrection is more than anticipating we will leave this world some day and go to heaven. Rather, it is a bold confidence that God's kingdom, presence, and power are breaking into our world today and a whole new creation has begun.

✝ INTRODUCTION

The resurrection of Jesus is more than a belief that his body was dead and came to life again, though this is quite true. It is an awareness that there was a cosmic explosion when Jesus rose again, and the power and repercussions of this reality echo through the ages to our day and into eternity.

From the earliest years of the church, followers of Jesus were uniform in their affirmation and confidence that Jesus had raised, bodily, from the dead. He had come through death, out the other side, and a new reality was born. The tomb was empty! The risen Jesus had met with them, taught them, shared meals, and instructed them. The one who had died on the cross was alive again.

Because Jesus has risen, we have more than confidence that our eternity is secure. We have an invitation to become his ambassadors in the world today. Through his church, Jesus wants to bring justice, lift up beauty, and lavish his gifts on the earth. And the primary way he plans to do this is through you and me.

> The eternal expression of the father's love became the incarnate expression of the father's love so that by his self-giving to death, even the death of the cross, the whole creation can be reconciled to God.

✝ TALK ABOUT IT

When you think of believers being resurrected someday, how do you picture this in your mind?

> Jesus' resurrection is the beginning of that new life, the fresh grass growing through the concrete of corruption and decay in the old world. That final redemption will be the moment when heaven and earth are joined together at last, in a burst of God's creative energy for which Easter is the prototype and source.

✝ DVD TEACHING NOTES

As you watch the DVD teaching segment for session two, featuring N. T. Wright, use the following outline to record anything that stands out to you.

First-century beliefs about what happened to people when they died

- Ancient pagan views

- Ancient Jewish views

The early Christians were uniform in their belief in the resurrection

Women play a significant role in the resurrection narratives

Portraits of Jesus in the resurrection stories

Something new is going on and two things had to have happened

Jesus had done something new

God's new creation had already begun

Our calling is to be advance foretastes of that new creation

The first Christians did not simply believe in life after death; they virtually never spoke simply of going to heaven when they died. When they did speak of heaven as a postmortem destination, they seemed to regard this heavenly life as a temporary stage on the way to the eventual resurrection of the body.

✝ DVD DISCUSSION

1. N. T. Wright notices that people tend to say conservative things at a graveside ... they stick to what they were told when they were young. How have you seen this? Why do you think people who are not particularly devout or serious about faith say things at someone's passing that do not reflect what they seem to believe and live the rest of the time?

2. When we read the gospel accounts of the resurrection from Matthew, Mark, Luke, and John, each tells the story in distinct and varied ways. How does this lend support for the authority of these accounts?

3. The women play a striking role in the resurrection narratives, yet in the first century women were not seen as credible witnesses. How does this actually support the gospel accounts of the resurrection?

> From the start within early Christianity it was built in as part of the belief in resurrection that the new body, though it will certainly be a body in the sense of a physical object occupying space and time, will be a transformed body, a body whose material, created from the old material, will have new properties.

4. **Read:** John 20:19–20. When Christ is raised, he appears to be both familiar, yet altogether different. How is Jesus different after the resurrection?

5. Some people look at the resurrection this way: "Jesus died, he was raised, and now we get to go to heaven!" Wright suggests another way to see the resurrection: "It is about a new bodily life *in* this world and *for* this world. God's new creation has begun and we have a job to do. The resurrection empowers us

to live in new ways today." How might these two viewpoints send believers in quite different directions in their daily lives?

> Resurrection is not an absurd event within the old world but the symbol and starting point of the new world. The claim advanced in Christianity is of that magnitude: Jesus of Nazareth ushers in not simply a new religious possibility, not simply a new ethic or a new way of salvation, but a new creation.

6. Wright declares that our calling is to be "advance foretastes of the new creation!" What is a practical way you can seek to be God's "advanced foretaste" in *one* of these places:

  • In your home

  • In your workplace

  • In your community

7. The power of Easter is more than just a promise of eternal life in heaven some day in the future (though this is part of it). If the church gets this truth, what are specific ways this shift in thinking could transform the way we interact with the world?

8. In ancient Palestine, water was life! Our lives are to be like that. Tell about a person you know who seems to naturally bring the refreshing life of God's living water wherever they go. What sorts of things does this person do that reflect the resurrected presence of Jesus?

9. God wants to flood the dry, dusty world around us with the refreshing water of his presence. What is one thing you can personally do this coming week to bring the refreshing flood of God's presence, love, and compassion to a dry place you travel regularly?

> The empty tomb and the meetings with Jesus are as well established as any historical data could expect to be. They are, in combination, the only possible explanation for the stories and beliefs that grew up so quickly among Jesus' followers.

10. Wright talks about artistic creativity and expressions of beauty. We can bring these things through our passion for justice, through our tenderness to the needy, and through our acts of kindness to the marginalized. If you have not already discussed with your group a project or ministry you could do together to bring beauty to your community, unleash justice for someone who is oppressed, or show compassion to a hurting person, do so now.

If your group has time, you may choose to watch the bonus section of the DVD for session two now. (If not, consider viewing it on your own or as a group as part of your between-sessions activities.) Here are some reflection questions for the bonus section:

Most people in the biblical world saw heaven and earth as over-lapping and interlocking spheres of reality. They believed that God's world could touch our world at any time. What are signs you see that God is closer than we sometimes recognize?

The sovereignty of Jesus did not come with displays of power, but through love, service, humility, and eventually his sacrificial death. How should this reality inform the way we seek to bring his presence into our spheres of influence?

Jesus sent his followers out to do the same kinds of things that he had done for people. What is one thing Jesus did that you know he wants you to begin doing?

✝ CLOSING PRAYER

Take time as a group to pray in some of the following directions:

- Thank God that Jesus is truly risen and alive today.
- Pray for power to be God's ambassador of the resurrected presence of Jesus wherever you go in the coming week.
- Thank God for the people he has placed in your life who have brought living water and the presence of Jesus.
- Pray for your church to be a body of people who are so connected to the risen Jesus that they reflect his presence in the world as they seek justice, bear God's love, and bring beauty alive in the world around them.

Hope is what you get when you suddenly realize that a different worldview is possible.... The same worldview shift that is demanded by the resurrection of Jesus is the shift that will enable us to transform the world.

✝
BETWEEN SESSIONS

Personal Reflection

In a moment when you are feeling thirsty, even parched, get a cold glass of water and drink it slowly. Allow yourself to feel the refreshment that comes from this simple gift. Then, remember that Jesus calls you to be his living water in this world. Think about how the risen Jesus quenches your thirst and satisfies your soul. Then, reflect on places you will be in the coming days ... places that can be dry, arid, and desolate. While you are drinking your water, ask God to give you creative ideas for how he might bring his refreshment to these places through your words, actions, and presence.

Personal Action

Take a walk through a cemetery. Read some of the tombstones and reflect on what kind of theology is being expressed. In the quietness of this place, ask the Holy Spirit of God to let your life be a testimony to the resurrection of Jesus.

Group Engagement

Wright talked about how each part of the body of Christ has a different function and contributes something valuable (1 Corinthians 12). In the coming times your group gathers for this study, talk about how God has gifted each of you and think about how these varied spiritual gifts can function together to bring the resurrected presence of Jesus more fully into the life of your local church. What can you each contribute, in the setting of your church, to bring the presence and love of the resurrected Jesus alive in the community of believers?

Prayer Direction

- Pray that you will embrace and create beauty that will reflect the presence of the risen Christ.
- Ask for eyes to see and notice moments when you can let the living water of Jesus flow from you into the lives of others.
- Pray for your local church to become a source of resurrection power in your community.
- Thank Jesus for unleashing his resurrection presence in your heart, home, church, and this world.

Recommended Reading

In preparation for session three, you may want to read chapters 5–7 of the book *Surprised by Hope*, by N. T. Wright.

Journal, Reflections, and Notes

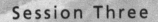

THE HOPE OF HEAVEN

Heaven is not a far away place we hope to go some day. Through Christ it is very near, it is the control room of earth, and as we follow Jesus, the reality of heaven comes alive in us and is unleashed through us.

✝ INTRODUCTION

Heaven will not be a boring place, off in distant space, where we play harps, sit on clouds, and sing the same stanza of the same song forever. Heaven is God's space, filled with peace, justice, and beauty. Heaven and earth are overlapping realities and the resurrection of Jesus has connected these two spheres more closely than we know.

Heaven is the control room of earth and God's sovereign rule is present today. As we learn to walk with Jesus and live as God's people in this world, the kingdom plan of God continues to unfold and be revealed. We are not waiting to fly off to heaven one day, but heaven is breaking into our present circumstances with each passing moment. If we pay close attention, we will see that heaven and earth are overlapping today.

One of the ways God brings his kingdom, "on earth as it is in heaven," is through his people. You and I are invited to be vehicles God can use to bring his love, justice, and beauty to a world desperate for all of these things. The hope of heaven is not something we are waiting for, but it is what we enter each day as we follow Jesus and let his heavenly plans unfold in us.

> What God did for Jesus on the first Easter Day, he has promised to do for each one who is in Christ, each one indwelt by the Spirit of Christ. That is the biblical and historic Christian expectation in terms of ourselves as human beings.

✝ TALK ABOUT IT

A *Far Side* cartoon once depicted a guy on a cloud, playing a harp, and saying, "I wish I'd brought a magazine." The implication is that heaven will be boring. What other pictures of heaven are part of the cultural consciousness, and what do you think causes people to view heaven in these terms?

> So far from sitting on clouds playing harps, as people often imagine, the redeemed people of God in the new world will be the agents of his love going out in new ways to accomplish new creative tasks to celebrate and extend the glory of his love.

✝ DVD TEACHING NOTES

As you watch the DVD teaching segment for session three, featuring N. T. Wright, use the following outline to record anything that stands out to you.

The common view of heaven as being far away ... therefore God is far away

Biblical view: Heaven and earth are interlocking spheres of God's creation ... they work together

Heaven as the control room for what happens on earth (God's sovereignty)

Jesus as the ultimate place where heaven and earth meet

Place of the temple for Jewish people

Heaven and hell as states of existence that are not the same

What does being truly human look like?

The kingdom of heaven and the kingdom of God

Jesus teaches us to pray

Heaven and God's rule coming on earth (God's space and our space coming together)

> What creation needs is neither abandon nor evolution but rather redemption and renewal; and this is both promised and guaranteed by the resurrection of Jesus from the dead.... The whole world is waiting, on tiptoe with expectation, for the moment when that resurrection life and power sweeps through it, filling it with the glory of God as the waters cover the sea.

✝ DVD DISCUSSION

1. A Russian cosmonaut came back from space and declared, "I looked for God and did not find him. No God, no heaven, no nothing!" How might a Christian respond to such a statement?

2. How might viewing heaven as a place very far away and a reality entirely separate from us have a harmful impact on the way we pray and relate to God?

> The method of the kingdom will match the message of the kingdom. The kingdom will come as the church, energized by the Spirit.

3. In the Bible, heaven and earth are the two interlocking spheres of God's good creation. Tell about a time you really felt heaven and the presence of God was near you, overlapping into this world.

4. **Read:** Ephesians 1:7–10. What do you learn about the connection and overlap of heaven and earth in this passage?

5. Heaven and earth don't just overlap, but heaven is the control room of what happens on earth. Kings and rulers can claim to run this world, but God has his hands on the controls! What is one situation in your life where you need to be reminded of God's sovereign rule to strengthen you and give you hope?

6. N. T. Wright is clear that the message of Jesus is not simply about keeping people from ending up in hell. It is also more than helping them "go to heaven." How have you seen people reduce the life and gospel of Jesus to a simple message about a person's future destination?

Death as we now know it is the last enemy, not a good part of the good creation; and therefore death must be defeated if the life-giving God is to be honored as the true lord of the world. When this has happened, and only then, Jesus the Messiah, the Lord of the world, will hand over the rule of the kingdom to his father, and God will be all in all.

7. Wright warns against using the possibility of hell to frighten people "into heaven." He says this approach can appeal to wrong instincts that are based on self-preservation and selfishness. How have you seen people use hell as a scare tactic, and what are some possible results of this approach?

8. Wright says we should not look at heaven and hell as locations in our cosmos (heaven way up in the sky, hell down in the middle of the earth) but as states of existence. "In the light of heaven we become truly human. The point of hell is that people become less human ... because we become like the things we worship." How does this understanding of heaven and hell resonate with you?

9. **Read:** Matthew 6:9 – 10. Wright believes this prayer helps us see that the kingdom of heaven is not a place where we go to escape *from* earth, but the rule and reign of God coming into human history and *onto* the earth! How is this a new way of thinking? What are signs we can see that reveal heaven is coming to earth today?

10. We are to pray, "Your kingdom come...." What can we do to help the kingdom of God enter into our daily lives in *one* of these areas?

- In our homes

- In our neighborhoods

- In our workplaces

- In our churches

The real problem with the myth of progress is that it cannot deal with evil. And when I say, "deal with," I don't just mean intellectually, though that is true as well; I mean in practice. It can't develop a strategy that actually addresses the severe problems of evil in the world. This is why all the evolutionary optimism of the last two hundred years remains helpless before world war, drug crime, Auschwitz, apartheid, child pornography, and the other interesting sidelines that evolution has thrown up for our entertainment in the twentieth century.

If your group has time, you may choose to watch the bonus section of the DVD for session three now. (If not, consider viewing it on your own or as a group as part of your between-sessions activities.) Here are some reflection questions for the bonus section:

A positive article written in response to N. T. Wright's book *Surprised by Hope* was unfortunately (and in error) titled, "New Bishop Abolishes Heaven and the Soul!" In light of some Christians' understanding of heaven, hell, and the soul, can you explain why the article and the title caused confusion?

Read: 1 Timothy 6:13 – 16. How does this passage speak to the idea that God is immortal, and what implications does it have on the claim some people make that human beings have "immortal souls"?

Read: 1 Corinthians 15:50 – 54. Wright is emphatic that God gives immortality to those who are in Christ. It is *given* — we don't possess it on our own! How does this fly in the face of the common belief that all people have immortal souls?

✝ CLOSING PRAYER

Take time as a group to pray in some of the following directions:

- Thank God that heaven will be vibrant, alive, dynamic, and more interesting than we can dream!
- Give praise to Jesus for connecting heaven and earth closely through his resurrection.
- Pray that you will see and feel how heaven is breaking into this life and how God is sovereign and at the controls of this earth ... even when things might seem confusing and troubling.

> Redemption is not simply making creation a bit better, as the optimistic evolutionist would try to suggest. Nor is it rescuing spirits and souls from an evil material world, as the Gnostic would want to say. It is the remaking of creation, having dealt with the evil that is defacing and distorting it. And it is accomplished by the same God, now known in Jesus Christ, through whom it was made in the first place.

Corruptah —

Death is swallowed up in Victory

✝
BETWEEN SESSIONS

Personal Reflection

Heaven is the control room of earth. God is on the throne and through the life, death, and resurrection of Jesus, the sovereign rule of God is coming into this world in greater and greater measure. Humbly examine your own life. Is there an area you are resisting God's control and leadership? How are you fighting the invitation to surrender this area of your life? How might your life be different if you let this attitude or action come under the control of God's heavenly rule?

Personal Action

Take a step forward in surrendering your life more fully to the lordship of Jesus. In the "Personal Reflection" section above you identified an area of your life where you are clinging to the controls of some action or attitude that you know God wants you to surrender to him. What can you do in the coming days to change this pattern in your life and bring it into alignment with God's way of living? Pray for the power of the resurrected Christ to fill you so that you can live in a new way ... one that pleases Jesus.

Group Engagement

N. T. Wright talks about how our worship space and church services can give us pictures of how heaven and earth connect. Plan to attend a worship service with your group sometime in the coming weeks. Then linger in the worship space for fifteen to twenty minutes afterward to talk about how you felt and saw heaven and earth coming together in that service. Look around the worship space and identify symbols, structures, and furnishings that help you picture how heaven is very near us. Finally, pray together to thank Jesus for all he has done to bridge this glorious heaven-and-earth experience we have.

Prayer Direction

- Pray that God's sovereign rule would be seen and felt on this earth.
- Thank Jesus that his resurrection makes it possible for heaven and earth to overlap. Thank God for the privilege of worship and pray for fresh experiences of heaven intersecting with earth as you gather to worship with God's people.
- Pray for people in your life who have never embraced Jesus and his kingdom. Pray that they will open their hearts to the Savior and his glorious heaven-and-earth plan for all people.
- Ask for the Spirit of God to use you, each day, to be a conduit of God's kingdom life to the places you travel.

Recommended Reading

In preparation for session four, you may want to read chapters 8 and 9 of the book *Surprised by Hope*, by N. T. Wright.

Journal, Reflections, and Notes

_____

_____

_____

_____

_____

_____

_____

_____

_____

_____

_____

_____

_____

_____

_____

_____

_____

_____

THE HOPE OF JESUS' SECOND COMING

The hope of the second coming is based on the biblical confidence that Jesus will one day return to this world, restore creation, heal his people, and make all things new.

† INTRODUCTION

Jesus Christ died on the cross, was buried for three days, and then rose again in glory. He started something entirely new ... the kingdom of God was breaking into human history. Since that time, the church has stood as a signpost for all who will look and see. Heaven intersects with earth and God is building his kingdom.

Now, the church and all of creation awaits the return of Jesus and the final consummation of his work here on earth. This is the hope of the second coming. It is not about God sweeping down and scooping up his people to rescue us from a dying planet. Rather, it is about Jesus returning to redeem the earth, heal his people, sort out all that is wrong, and reign in glory.

As we wait for that day, we are not to spend our time peering into the sky wondering when Jesus will arrive. We are not to create fanciful scenarios about how Jesus will come. Instead, we are to invest our energy and time in caring for his creation, loving each other, sharing his grace, seeking justice, celebrating beauty, and living with confidence that Jesus will return one day. Until that final consummation, we live each day with a profound awareness that Jesus is King of Kings and Lord of Lords.

> The word *eschatology*, which literally means "the study of the last things," doesn't just refer to death, judgment, heaven, and hell, as used to be thought. It also refers to the strongly held belief of most first-century Jews, and virtually all early Christians, that history was going somewhere under the guidance of God and that where it was going was toward God's new world of justice, healing, and hope.

✝ TALK ABOUT IT

Many people see the second coming of Jesus as an instant ticket out of this world. They don't anticipate his coming as a daily experience but solely as an event sometime in the future. How can our understanding of the second coming impact the way we act, live, and treat the world today?

> We must remind ourselves that all Christian language about the future is a set of signposts pointing into a mist. Signposts don't normally provide you with advance photographs of what you'll find at the end of the road, but that doesn't mean they aren't pointing in the right direction.

✝ DVD TEACHING NOTES

As you watch the DVD teaching segment for session four, featuring N. T. Wright, use the following outline to record anything that stands out to you.

Jesus began the task of launching the work of the kingdom

Biblical picture: Kingdom of God theology

Daniel 7, Acts, and Ephesians

The second coming: Jesus is going to sort it all out

Final judgment

God is sorting out the good news through Jesus (Romans 2 and 2 Corinthians 5)

1 Thessalonians 4

Jesus is King of Kings

Theology of the second coming

There will come a time, which might indeed come at any
time, when, in the great renewal of the world that Easter
itself foreshadowed, Jesus himself will be personally present
and will be the agent and model of the transformation that
will happen both to the whole world and also to believers.

✝ DVD DISCUSSION

1. In the Apostles' Creed we read that Jesus will come again to
    "judge the living and the dead." What do you think this means?

2. Wright talks about "the rapture" of the church, an idea that is
    quite popular among some groups of Christians. If you have
    been exposed to this idea, briefly summarize it and explain what
    people who anticipate a rapture are waiting for.

3. **Read:** Acts 1:7–8 and Acts 2:1–4. How does the coming of the Holy Spirit into individual lives, the church, and the world buttress the belief that God is on a mission to bring heaven and earth together?

4. How have you experienced the Holy Spirit's power and presence in ways that point to the reality of God's heavenly kingdom breaking into this world?

5. **Read:** Daniel 7:13–14 and Mark 13:24–27. Many people see these passages as an affirmation that Jesus will come on the clouds and take his people out of the world. How does Wright portray what is happening in these passages in a very different light?

> The picture of Jesus as the coming judge is the central feature of another absolutely vital and nonnegotiable Christian belief: that there will indeed be a judgment in which the creator God will set the world right once and for all....

> We need to remind ourselves that throughout the Bible, not
> least in the Psalms, God's coming judgment is a good thing,
> something to be celebrated, longed for, yearned over.

6. **Read:** Acts 1:9–11. The second coming of Jesus is a biblical belief and very important. N. T. Wright puts it this way: "If we don't hold to the belief in the second coming of Jesus, we have not rounded out the whole kingdom of God theology." What do we lose if we do not embrace confidence in the second coming of Jesus?

7. **Read:** Philippians 3:20–21. The apostle Paul writes about Jesus "bringing everything under his control." Wright talks about how the judgment God will bring is about sorting things out, making them right, and bringing them under his sovereign rule. How does Wright's understanding of "judgment" line up with how you have been taught to understand it?

> Because we live between ascension and appearing, joined
> to Jesus Christ by the Spirit but still awaiting his final coming
> and presence, we can be both properly humble *and* properly
> confident. "We proclaim not ourselves, but Jesus Christ as
> Lord, and ourselves as your servants through Jesus."

8. **Read:** 1 Thessalonians 5:1–8. What are some of the metaphors in this passage and how is Paul mixing them? What warning does Wright give about passages that use this kind of imagery (including 1 Thessalonians 4:13–18)?

9. Wright looks at some of the political and social implications of our theology of the second coming. What does he say happens if we embrace the idea of a rapture where all the faithful followers of Jesus are swept off the earth? What does he say about embracing the idea that Jesus will come to earth as the King of Kings and the Lord of Lords?

10. One day Jesus will bring perfect justice, peace, and wisdom to this earth. Until that day, as his kingdom is coming, we are responsible to bring these things in Jesus' name. What is one practical way you can be an agent of *one* of the following things right where you will be this coming week?

    • Justice in a world that can be very unfair

    • Peace in a broken and conflict-filled world

- Wisdom when people often settle for shallow answers

> The one through whom God's justice will finally sweep the world is not a hard-hearted, arrogant, or vengeful tyrant but rather the Man of Sorrows, who was acquainted with grief; the Jesus who loved sinners and died for them; the Messiah who took the world's judgment upon himself on the cross.

If your group has time, you may choose to watch the bonus section of the DVD for session four now. (If not, consider viewing it on your own or as a group as part of your between-sessions activities.) Here are some reflection questions for the bonus section:

Roman citizens who lived far from the city of Rome knew that they were obligated to bring the heart, vision, and life of Rome wherever they were. What will help followers of Jesus live with a growing daily awareness that we are to bring the heart, vision, and life of heaven to this earth ... right where God has put us?

We are residents of earth, but we are called to bring the culture of heaven into this world. We are to be so soaked in God's way of seeing the world that we can't help but bring the values and agendas of heaven to our homes, neighborhoods, society, and everywhere we go! What are some of "heaven's agendas" that God wants to weave into the fabric of this world, and what can you do this week to partner with God in helping this become a reality?

✝ CLOSING PRAYER

Take time as a group to pray in some of the following directions:

- Pray that you will live with a sober awareness that Jesus will return in glory and victory one day!
- Ask for strength to care for the world that Jesus made and will return to restore.
- There are many varied views when it comes to end times and the second coming of Jesus. (You might even find that your view of the second coming is quite different than that of N. T. Wright.) These are not issues worth fighting over and they should certainly not divide us as followers of Jesus. Pray for a humble heart about your beliefs on this topic and ask for the Spirit to spare you from being contentious or prideful as you interact with those who have a different perspective.
- Celebrate that Jesus is King of Kings and Lord of Lords, and lift him up as the ruler of heaven and earth!

When I (and many others) use the word *eschatology*, we don't simply mean the second coming, still less a particular theory about it; we mean, rather, the entire sense of God's future for the world and the belief that that future has already begun to come forward to meet us in the present.

†

BETWEEN SESSIONS

Personal Reflection

One of the topics N. T. Wright touched on was the awareness that Jesus is Lord and Caesar is not! This is an invitation to bow the knee to Jesus and always remember that whoever is on the throne, in office, or in a place of political influence is not really the final authority in the universe or the world. At the same time, the apostle Paul is clear that we are to respect and pray for those who are in places of authority and governmental leadership (Romans 13:1; Titus 3:1). How are you doing at striking a God-honoring balance of praying for and respecting those in political leadership but also making sure you only bow your knees to Jesus?

Personal Action

The King of Kings, Jesus, is on the throne and one day he will return and make all things right. When you know this, you can pray in new ways. Make a list of some of your local and national leaders. (You might need to search online, but these names are easy to find.) Commit to begin praying for these people in the coming weeks. Whether they are Christians or not, pray that they will lead in a way that will honor God and bring justice to their places of influence.

Group Engagement

Jesus will return to this world and he will sort things out and make them right. Until then, we are called to be stewards of his beautiful creation. As a group, identify some kind of service project you can do to care for God's creation and make his beauty known. It could be spending a weekend morning cleaning a river, local park, or roadside. It could be a decision to volunteer with your city and ask what you can do to beautify your community. It might be plant-ing flowers or new plants on your church campus (with permission, of course). As you do this work, commit to pray that people will see beauty that points to God's creative power. Pray also that you would all live with an awareness that God made the world, asks us to care for it, and Jesus will return one day to sort things out and make all things new.

Prayer Direction

- Pray that your understanding of Christ's return is shaped by Scripture.
- Ask God to direct your steps so that you will live in ways that will show the world that Jesus is here today, and com-ing in glory.
- Pray for wisdom as you vote, work for justice, and serve in your community.
- Pray that Christians with differing views of the end times will not compromise their witness to the world by quibbling and arguing.

Recommended Reading

In preparation for session five, you may want to read chapters 10–12 of the book *Surprised by Hope*, by N. T. Wright.

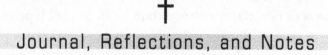

Journal, Reflections, and Notes

_____

_____

_____

_____

_____

_____

_____

_____

_____

_____

_____

_____

_____

_____

_____

_____

_____

_____

_____

_____

_____

THE HOPE OF
SALVATION

Through the resurrection of Jesus Christ, we are saved from sin and death. But, there is more to the story. God is saving and restoring all of creation and he invites us into this work of sorting out what is wrong in the world.

✝ INTRODUCTION

Jesus offers salvation from sin, death, and the evil of this world. At the same time, his salvation is a call to something. We are saved *from* sin and *for* good works. Just as Jesus is sorting out the brokenness in our lives and the world, we are called to help him in his work of putting things right in our lives, society, and even in the created order.

This process of God putting things right includes not only his saving power, but also God's righteous judgment. The judgment of Jesus is not simply condemnation of what is wrong in the world. It is also his justice being unleashed to make things right.

One of the primary ways God is revealing both his salvation and righteous judgment in the world today is through his people. Like a mirror, we reflect the presence of God and his image in life's daily encounters. When we do this, both the salvation and judgment of Jesus are made manifest.

God is not perched off on some heavenly throne, sitting on his hands and waiting to battle evil and sort out the wrong in the world at some future time. He is entering human history each and every day through you and me. Salvation and judgment are coming today as we lock horns with evil, battle against sin, and become agents of God's new creation right where he places us.

> The work of salvation, in its full sense, is 1) about whole human beings, not merely souls; 2) about the present, not simply the future; and 3) about what God does through us, not merely what God does in and for us.

✝ TALK ABOUT IT

God is a refuge! But if we see our faith as primarily a safe place to escape the turmoil of life and the church as a retreat from the world, this has serious implications. What are some of the potentially negative consequences of Christians spending most of their energy retreating and running from the world?

> The point of resurrection, as Paul has been arguing throughout 1 Corinthians 15, is that the present bodily life is not valueless just because it will die. God will raise it to new life. What you do with your body in the present matters because God has a great future in store for it.

✝ DVD TEACHING NOTES

As you watch the DVD teaching segment for session five, featuring N. T. Wright, use the following outline to record anything that stands out to you.

What is salvation?

- Technically

- Biblically

Salvation and judgment belong together

God's promise to sort the whole world out

The Messiah as God's agent, Psalm 2:7–9

Biblical vision of humankind: Made in the image of God

Picture of God sorting out the world through the Messiah

The resurrection of Jesus and of God's people, 1 Corinthians 15

Vision of new creation, Ephesians 2:8–10

> Forget those images about lounging around playing harps.
> There will be work to do and we shall relish doing it. All
> the skills and talents we have put to God's service in this
> present life—and perhaps too the interests and likings we
> gave up because they conflicted with our vocation—will be
> enhanced and ennobled and given back to us to be exer-
> cised to his glory.

✝ DVD DISCUSSION

1. The word *salvation* means "rescue," being delivered from something! But in biblical terms, it is not just about being saved *from*
   something but being saved *for* something. When you think of
   salvation, what are we saved *from* and what are we saved *for*?

2. **Read:** Romans 8:18–25. The biblical vision of salvation is not
   just about us being saved. What does the apostle Paul mean
   when he says that the whole creation will be saved?

3. In most people's church experience they are taught that salvation and judgment are polar opposites. N. T. Wright says this is

not the case. What do you think Wright is getting at when he says that salvation and judgment are similar?

4. **Read:** Acts 17:22–32. When Jesus was raised from the dead on that first Easter, it was a sign of God's power to sort things out! God passed judgment on all the sin of the world. It was as if God was saying, "This is what I will do for the whole world some day and Jesus is the one through whom I will do it!" How is Jesus the one through whom all our messes can be sorted out and all of our sins cleansed?

> God is utterly committed to set the world right in the end. This doctrine, like that of resurrection itself, is held firmly in place by the belief in God as creator, on the one side, and the belief in his goodness, on the other.

5. When God created the world, he put people here to reflect his image and wise order. How can believers reflect the glory, presence, and image of God into the dark and confused places of this world?

6. As you think of the life of Jesus, what are some specific things about the way he lived that show he was the perfect human being? What are examples of things he did that point to what we should do?

> The risen Jesus is both the model for the Christian's future body and the means by which it comes about.

7. **Read:** 1 Corinthians 15:21–28. Paul talks about Jesus' resurrection and our own. Until this final consummation, we are in a cosmic battle with evil. What are some of the ways Christians should battle the evil systems in our world?

8. In the resurrection of Jesus is the announcement that God has already won the battle. How might we face the pain, struggle, and evil in this world differently if we lived with confident assurance that Jesus has already assured the victory over them?

9. **Read:** 2 Corinthians 5:17–21. What does it mean to be God's new creation, and what is one way you can live out this "new-creation life" in the coming weeks?

10. **Read:** Ephesians 2:8–10. God's people are not saved *by* good works but saved *for* good works! How might your life look different in *one* of the following areas if you committed to do good works, for the glory of God, on a regular basis?

- In your marriage

- In your workplace

- In your local church

- In your neighborhood

- In someplace else you go regularly

11. Wright suggests that Christians should be people who: make the world come alive, bring texture and color, create art, write books, open new possibilities, infuse joy, instill love, bring hope. What are some ways you see Christians doing this? What are some fresh new ways we can bring this kind of God-breathed goodness into the world?

Salvation is not "going to heaven" but "being raised in life in God's new heaven and new earth."

If your group has time, you may choose to watch the bonus section of the DVD for session five now. (If not, consider viewing it on your own or as a group as part of your between-sessions activities.) Here are some reflection questions for the bonus section:

Wright draws some clear distinctions between Platonic thought and biblical thinking. What are some of the differences?

According to Hebrew thought (contained in the Old Testament), how does God view creation and all the material things we see, touch, taste, and smell? Why is it important that we see the world the way God does?

✝ CLOSING PRAYER

Take time as a group to pray in some of the following directions:

- Thank God for his protecting hand over you in times of need and struggle.
- Ask Jesus to reflect his presence through your life into specific places you will walk in the coming week.
- Thank God for the hope that one day he will sort out all that is wrong in our lives and the world.
- Surrender your schedule and abilities to God and invite him to use you to sort out wrong things in the world around you.

BETWEEN SESSIONS

Personal Reflection

N. T. Wright talks about three things that can happen through us when we are operating as agents of God's new created order:

- We can bring God's healing to the world.
- We can offer wise and creative judgment.
- We can exercise discernment.

In which of these areas do you need to grow and develop? What steps can you take to increase your commitment to be someone who helps bring this new created order to fruition in the world?

Personal Action

Wright talked about "locking horns with evil." This can involve speaking up, resisting, taking action, and praying. Identify a specific evil or injustice that is happening right in your local community. It could be people going hungry amid plenty of food, children not getting good medical care, domestic abuse, or a host of other evils. Commit to pray for God's just judgment against this evil. Also, let God know that you want to be a mirror reflecting his presence and care in this situation. Try to identify one action you can take in the coming week that will reflect God's presence and image into this area of injustice.

Group Engagement

Commit to gather as a group for the express purpose of writing letters or emails to communicate your concern about injustices happening in your community or country. Seek to be clear about your concern and constructive in what you write. As you send off your letters, pray that your voice will be heard and God's justice will be done.

Prayer Direction

- Pray for the day that creation will be set free and restored, and commit to care for and nurture God's world until that day comes.
- Thank Jesus for being a righteous judge and the author of our salvation.
- Confess where your life is not reflecting the image and glory of God, and repent of these life patterns and behaviors.
- Ask God for the power you need to lock horns with the evil in this world and battle against it in the name of Jesus.

Recommended Reading

In preparation for session six, you may want to read chapters 13–15 of the book *Surprised by Hope*, by N. T. Wright.

Journal, Reflections, and Notes

_____

_____

_____

_____

_____

_____

_____

_____

_____

_____

_____

_____

_____

_____

_____

_____

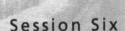

THE HOPE OF THE CHURCH

The hope of the church is more than what lies ahead some day when Jesus returns. It is our experience of God's kingdom breaking into our everyday journey of faith as we do justice, extend mercy, express love, offer compassion, and celebrate beauty ... all in the name of Jesus.

✝ INTRODUCTION

It is easy to look at our life and the small contribution one person can offer and wonder if we can make a difference. Like one stone in a large cathedral, we can seem small and inconsequential, to ourselves and sometimes to others. But God does not see us this way. In the heart of God, we are partners in bringing his hope to the world.

It is not up to us to build the kingdom, but we can build *for* the kingdom. As resurrection people who know that heaven and earth overlap, we can become agents of God's beauty in a world that needs a song, a beautiful painting, a new dance, or a heart-touching poem. We can also stand for justice in a world where injustice seems to have a vise grip on so many people.

The resurrection of Jesus does not move us to a passive and sedentary life of waiting for God to show up some day in the distant future. The hope of the resurrection inspires and empowers Christians to stand strong, work hard, pray more fervently, and live with compassion. As the power of the resurrection fills our hearts, homes, and churches, we stand firm, we let nothing move us, we always give ourselves fully to the work of the Lord, because we know our labor is not in vain!

"Therefore, my dear brothers, stand firm. Let nothing move you. Always give yourselves fully to the work of the Lord, because you know that your labor in the Lord is not in vain" (1 Corinthians 15:58).

✝ TALK ABOUT IT

Every Christian offers their part, their small contribution, to the work of God in this world. What is one way God is using you to bring his kingdom plan alive?

> If we are engaging in the work of new creation, in seeking to bring advance signs of God's eventual new world into being in the present, in justice and beauty and a million other ways, then at the center of the picture stands the personal call of the gospel of Jesus to every child, woman, and man.

✝ DVD TEACHING NOTES

As you watch the DVD teaching segment for session six, featuring N. T. Wright, use the following outline to record anything that stands out to you.

Paul's ending exhortation in 1 Corinthians 15:58

God will transform and reaffirm

Getting on with your work: new creation

- Justice: We need to be campaigners for justice ("Name it, shame it, and figure out a wise way of dealing with it.")

- Beauty: Brutalism and sentimentalism

Christian artists need a proper theology of resurrection and new creation

Paul's vision for creation to be set free, Romans 8

Justice and beauty come together in the work of evangelism

The impact of the church

> God intends his wise, creative, loving presence and power to
> be reflected—imaged, if you like—into his world through
> his human creatures.

✝ DVD DISCUSSION

1. **Read:** 1 Corinthians 15:50–58. It might seem that, after all of Paul's teaching on the resurrection, he would end this amazing argument with an invitation to relax and cruise our way into eternity. But he surprises us with a very different tone in verse 58. What exhortations does Paul give, and how should this stir our hearts and move us to action?

2. N. T. Wright says, "God is going to take everything in this present world that bears the mark of his love, goodness, power, and loving compassion and use it as the raw material out of which the new world will be made." What are some of these things God will use to form the new world?

3. What are some of the "little things" we do in this life and world that can often go unnoticed, but are very valuable in the scope of God building his kingdom now and forever?

4. **Read:** Micah 6:8. What are examples of how the church and Christians have worked for justice in the past and in the present? What are practical ways your church can join in this rich history of standing against injustice and for righteousness in your own community and in the world?

5. **Read:** Romans 8:19–25. What is the connection between resurrection and new creation and the ability to appreciate and celebrate beauty? What steps can the church take to embrace the beauty of the arts?

6. How can art, music, poetry, and other expressions of beauty help us hold together both pain and hope?

7. Wright talks about how the world can get a glimpse of the new things God is doing when they look at the church. If someone could get a clear picture of what is really happening in the life and heart of your local congregation, what picture would this paint in their mind? What would they learn about both the church and the heart of God?

> I believe that if we take justice, beauty, and evangelism in terms of the anticipation of God's eventual setting to rights of the whole world, we will find that they dovetail together and in fact that they are all part of the same larger whole, which is the message of hope and new life that comes with the good news of Jesus' resurrection.

8. What are some acts of justice we can do that will advance the cause of evangelism?

9. What are ways we can celebrate beauty, and how can this move Christians and the church forward in evangelism?

10. **Read:** Philippians 4:8 and Ephesians 3:10–12. Wright talks about how the church can build strategic partnerships as we do justice and celebrate beauty. What are ways your local church might partner in the pursuit of justice and/or beauty with *one* of the following:

- A local congregation

- A ministry or mission organization

- Some sort of civic group

- A group that celebrates beauty or seeks justice, but is not distinctively Christian

How might a partnership like this actually advance the cause of evangelism?

> The resurrection of Jesus and the gift of the Spirit mean that we are called to bring real and effective signs of God's renewed creation to birth even in the midst of the present age.

BONUS STUDY

If your group has time, you may choose to watch the bonus section of the DVD for session six now. (If not, consider viewing it on your own or as a group in the coming days.) Here are some reflection questions for the bonus section:

The apostle Paul wants us to remember that our "labor in the Lord is not in vain" (1 Corinthians 15:58). What are some things that cause us to become discouraged as we serve God, seek justice, and celebrate beauty? What can encourage us to keep giving ourselves fully to God's work, even when we feel discouraged?

God does not call us to do everything. But he does expect us to do our particular part in his work in this world. What is one way God has gifted and made you so that you can contribute to his plan for the church and this world?

✝ CLOSING PRAYER

Take time as a group to pray in some of the following directions:

- Thank God that even small acts of obedience bring him glory and make a difference in building his kingdom.
- Pray for the Christian artists you know to rightly reflect the glory of God through their particular medium.
- Pray for the church to embrace the beauty of the arts and invite artists to help in the process of gathered worship.
- Ask the Spirit to bring conviction into the heart of the church and individual Christians about the injustices that exist all around us.

> What we can and must do in the present, if we are obedient to the gospel, if we are following Jesus, and if we are indwelt, energized, and directed by the Spirit, is to build for the kingdom.

✝

IN THE COMING DAYS

Personal Reflection

Like the stonemason working on a small piece of a large building, we can feel as though our investment in the kingdom work of Christ is not terribly significant. Reflect back through the last couple years of your life. What are some of the contributions you have made? How has God used your contribution to forward the work of his kingdom? How have your little things become part of a larger movement of bringing God's heavenly kingdom to earth?

Personal Action

N. T. Wright talks about the importance of art in the life of a believer and in our community life as a church. Sometimes we miss this, but it is a sign of hope in this world and in our midst. In the coming weeks, invest some personal energy in some kind of artistic expression. You might play an instrument, but have not taken it out for some time. Find it, tune it up, and play! Try painting or pottery, write a poem, sing or dance. Ask the Holy Spirit to meet you in this artistic expression and allow you to experience the beauty of God.

Group Engagement

Christians sometimes miss the beauty of the arts or even shun them. Consider an outing with your group members to enjoy some kind of artistic beauty. You might attend a play, the ballet, an opera, the symphony, or an art gallery. After you have taken in the sights and sounds, debrief together about how you experienced beauty in this artistic expression. If you sensed God's presence or pleasure, talk about this as well. You might even want to chat about ways it could be appropriate to enfold more use of the arts in your church services.

Prayer Direction

- Thank God that he takes your little contributions and uses them for great kingdom causes.
- Pray that you will learn to notice injustice around you and take action against it with a Spirit-led passion.
- Pray that you will embrace beauty and support those who create art that inspires others and points them toward God.
- Ask the Holy Spirit to convict you any time you are tempted to put your feet up and take a passive posture rather than abounding in the work of the Lord.

†

Journal, Reflections, and Notes

_____

_____

_____

_____

_____

_____

_____

_____

_____

_____

_____

_____

_____

_____

_____

_____

_____

_____

Be sure to explore these other N.T. Wright titles:

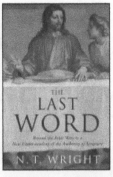

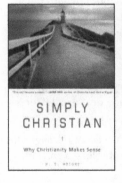

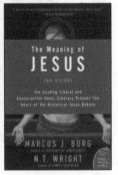

Available at your local bookstore.

HarperOne
An Imprint of HarperCollinsPublishers

Share Your Thoughts

With the Author: Your comments will be forwarded to the author when you send them to *zauthor@zondervan.com*.

With Zondervan: Submit your review of this book by writing to *zreview@zondervan.com*.

Free Online Resources at

www.zondervan.com

Zondervan AuthorTracker: Be notified whenever your favorite authors publish new books, go on tour, or post an update about what's happening in their lives at www.zondervan.com/authortracker.

Daily Bible Verses and Devotions: Enrich your life with daily Bible verses or devotions that help you start every morning focused on God. Visit www.zondervan.com/newsletters.

Free Email Publications: Sign up for newsletters on Christian living, academic resources, church ministry, fiction, children's resources, and more. Visit www.zondervan.com/newsletters.

Zondervan Bible Search: Find and compare Bible passages in a variety of translations at www.zondervanbiblesearch.com.

Other Benefits: Register yourself to receive online benefits like coupons and special offers, or to participate in research.

ZONDERVAN®

ZONDERVAN.com/
AUTHORTRACKER
follow your favorite authors